Opening Exercises

Tools for Navigating Life

Opening Exercises

Tools for Navigating Life

Three Voices

Illustrated by Maria Facci

Copyright © 2023 by Andrea Facci, Maria Facci, and Holly Lukens. All rights reserved

Publisher: Holly Lukens
1021 Puget St NE, Olympia, WA 98506

ISBN 978-0-9991107-4-4

No part of this publication may be reproduced, stored in a retrieval system, or transmitted, in any form or by any means, electronic or mechanical, photocopying, recording, or otherwise, without the prior permission of the publishers.

Cover photographs by Maria Facci

This book is dedicated to all of us everywhere as we try to know ourselves better.

Contents

Introduction: Cleaning out the Garage..................................1

Part I: Obstacles......................3

1. Not Being Heard: Why Bother Talking? 5
2. Not Being Seen: Invisible...........9
3. Autopilot Decisions................13
4. Not Trusting Others: Guarded...19
5. Not Belonging: Sidelined.........23
6. Gridlock: Stuck......................29
7. Controlled in a Relationship: Bound and Gagged..................33
8. Inadequate: Thinking We're Not Good Enough..........................37
9. Faking Good: Imposter............41

10. Feeling Out on a Limb: Exposed...................................45

11. Out of Breath: Being Overwhelmed.................................51

12. Cornerstones: Holding Up the World......................................55

13. Disappointment: Not Again...59

14. Grudge Holding....................65

15. Passing Up a Chance: Not Now...69

16. Trapped: No Way Out..........75

17. All My Fault: Blaming Ourselves.....................................79

18. Hedging: Am I Sure?..............83

19. Overdoing It: "No Problem".89

20. Life Is Flat.........................95

21. Influenza: Not Recognizing Our Influences..........................99

22. Overhelping..................105

23. Staying Seated: Inaction........109

24. Caving to Convenience.........115

25. Hitting a Wall: Facing Loss....119

26. I Believe...........................123

27. My Own Personal Obstacle..............................127

Part II: Core Issues and Exercises.129

A. Power and Control...............131

  1. Empathy Exercises.............131

  2. Releasing Control...............131

  3. Empowerment: Speaking Up.132

  4. Taking Control...................133

B. Boundaries..........................135

1. Respect for Others.............135

2. Wanting Your Own Way…....135

3. Self-Respect....................…..136

4. Coping With Intrusion…........136

5. Learning to Say No………....137

C. Old Habits and Leftovers….....139

   1. Leftovers: Boxes in the Basement……………………………...139

   2. Old Habits…………....….…..141

D. Self-Trust…..……………….....143

   1. Bad Decisions…………..…...143

   2. Staying Away From Decisions………………………...143

   3. Full Hand.......................…....144

E. Changing Limitations………...147

   Exploring Our Options…...……147

F. Avoidance......................151
  1. Having a Difficult Conversation......................151
  2. Dealing With an Awkward Situation......................152
  3. Change......................152
G. Making Choices......................153
  1. Present Choice......................153
  2. Past Choice......................154
H. Flexibility......................155
  1. Getting Dressed......................155
  2. Food for Thought......................156
I. Acceptance......................157
  1. What You've Done: Taking Responsibility......................157
  2. What You've Done: Seeing It Differently......................158

3. What Someone Else Has Done..................159

4. When No One Is to Blame for Harm or Loss......................160

J. Appreciating......................163

   1. Rethinking Appreciation....163

   2. Spreading Appreciation......165

   3. Simple Appreciation...........165

K. Clear Thinking....................167

   1. Be a Detective................168

   2. Check Your Sources..........170

   3. Be Careful......................171

Useful Resources....................173

Acknowledgments....................177

About Us..............................178

Index..................................179

Introduction

Cleaning out the Garage

Getting to know ourselves better is a lot like cleaning out a garage, or an attic or basement, or that overstuffed closet that rains down hats whenever we open it. We carry with us all our experiences and memories, everything we've said or done and everything that others have said and done to, for, and with us. It's easy to lose sight of who we are underneath all that.

We all have obstacles that interfere with our lives and keep us stuck.

Because three of us wrote this book, we see ourselves as Three Voices. We offer three different views of each obstacle discussed, but there are as many ways to approach this subject as there are people.

The book begins with the obstacles to knowing ourselves. Then it provides exercises based on core issues and designed to help deal with these obstacles. Please also see the list of useful resources at the back of the book.

We hope you find this book helpful, and we welcome your comments and suggestions.

Andrea Facci, Maria Facci, and Holly Lukens

Part I

Obstacles

Although an obstacle is usually thought of as a barrier that blocks our way, it may also turn out to be a benefit that unearths something important. Ask yourself, "Is this really an obstacle? If so, why do I think that, and what can I do about it?"

1

Not Being Heard

Why Bother Talking?

Andrea:

Not being heard feels like there is no room for what we say or might want to say. As large as the space, the group, the family—the chaos drowns us out. How strange that is. Chaos is the presence of so much activity, but one more voice, my voice would be too much. Silence would fall.

Maria:

I come from a loud and talkative family and I don't think any of us listen.

I am told to express myself but when I do I am dismissed.

I am able to talk to anybody. I have a lot of friends. I am outgoing and happy-go-lucky so no one wants to hear anything sad or bad from me.

I have no one to talk to, to tell my hopes, dreams, aspirations, loves, hates, likes, dislikes, funny moments, any part of my life to.

Holly:

"I am out with a few friends, and everyone is talking. When I try to join in, I am talked over or interrupted. No one seems to hear me."

"I make a suggestion at work, and it

goes unnoticed, but a coworker makes the same suggestion and is praised for it."

"Chris and I want a small wedding at a local park, but then Chris' mother invites all her friends and insists that we have the reception at a fancy hotel. We say no, but Chris later gives in and agrees to the hotel without asking me."

Those of us who are unheard may wonder why. Maybe we're just naturally quiet, but knowing that doesn't solve the problem. What would it be like to have friends who understand the give and take of a real conversation?

Would a different approach at work get

better results? Do I want to commit to someone who lets family members interfere in our marriage, dismisses my opinion, and shuts me out of a decision that affects us both?

> *There's a fine line between* assertiveness and aggression.

> *Starting Point*
> A: "We're having pizza for dinner."
> B: "I don't want pizza, thanks."
> A: "What toppings do you want?"
> B: "I'm not sure you heard me. I really don't want pizza for dinner. How about sandwiches instead?"

2

Not Being Seen

Invisible

Maria:

The woman who checked you out in the grocery store.

The garbage collectors.

The servers in restaurants.

The cashier at your gas station.

The people paving the road.

The homeless.

The people in your own home.

You.

Holly:

"I am standing at a counter to place a takeout order, and two people who come in after me are waited on first."

"At a community meeting, I raise my hand three times during question and answer period, but no one sees me, or at least no one calls on me."

"My brother and sister and I are together for an evening, and they start to talk about me as though I'm not there. When I call them on it, they deny doing it."

Invisibility is isolating. It's also annoying, but shoving people, screaming at meetings, or storming out of family dinners is not the answer, either. There must be a way to be more visible without acting like someone we're not.

Andrea:

I remember being a very enthusiastic student in grade school and raising my hand wildly because I knew the answer. I wanted someone, anyone really, to recognize that. I often wonder now whether I was proud of knowing the answer or terrified of being invisible. Maybe a little of both.

Sometimes it is comforting to know that the world is out there. People are somewhere doing normal things like starting the car or buying a bag of peas, looking at toys with their kids, picking out flowers for someone special or staring up at the clouds on a hot summer day. Their everydayness makes my day calmer and maybe a little more hopeful.

> *There's a fine line between* being present and being acknowledged.

> *Starting Point*
> "At the meeting, I raised my hand to make a comment, but nobody saw me. Do you mind if I run it by you so you can share it with the committee?"

3

Autopilot Decisions

Holly:

"This place has the best combination of housing and schools in our price range. It doesn't feel like home, but moving there makes the most sense."

"If they offer me the job, it would make sense to take it. The hours are long and so is the commute, but it pays more than I make now."

"We've been together for six years. Our families get along. Marriage makes sense."

We are human beings, not computers, and we need more than logic to get by.

Making major decisions without enthusiasm (or any other emotion, for that matter) can lead to empty choices that we may end up regretting. With good intentions and for reasons that make sense on paper, we can marry without passion, take a job that we know will make us miserable, or move somewhere we don't care about.

However, there are times when our only choice is the practical option. We can't always choose what we would prefer, but we can stay open to something better coming along later.

Making our best decisions requires a balance of reason and emotion, but that balance is sometimes out of reach.

Andrea:

When we were little, sometimes an adult would ask us to do something because they thought it would be safer for us and protect us from consequences. "Put on your jacket, it is cold outside" or "Look both ways before you cross the street." The translation of that was "I am teaching you to be sensible" so the adult felt caring and we felt cared for. Not having someone to tell us those things could be very confusing, in part because we could see so many others did have that in their lives. To help us find our balance, if we could, we imitated what we saw. As adults, others directing our lives is rarely a good idea. Often direction can be criticism spoken not out of love, not out of caring, but out of a wish to show power over our perceived incompetence. Direction was given under the appearance of protection or frustration: "You know you never load the dishwasher right," or "You know you hate to go there," or "Why would you want to do that? We have too much to do here—you would think you would know that—why don't you know that?" This shaming would be bad enough if directed at a child, but it is about shaming the adult into compliance. You are only as good as I decide you are.

Maria:

No need to think about it. Just react the same as always and do what is needed. No reason to start "thinking" about things. It just gets you in trouble. No need to stir things up. I have always done it this way and there's no need to change now.

> *There's a fine line between* common sense and settling for less.

Starting Point

Making a major decision involves more than a list of pros and cons. It may look like a perfect decision on paper, but don't let that override your intuition.

4

Not Trusting Others

Guarded

Andrea:

There are times when feeling guarded is like looking through tiny holes in the wall of a fortress: "Is it safe?" " How safe is it?" "How can I be sure?" There is so much weight in those questions, so many filters. Like wearing wet clothes, and being forced on a long journey. There is a lot to carry. We just make sure we don't show it.

Maria:

Who to trust. How to trust.

People make it impossible.

You have seen how they are, who they've betrayed, how much they talk, how they say one thing and do another. It is impossible to feel safe with them. Any of them. No way, no how, no one.

Holly:

"I can't always depend on other people."

"Is there some secret way to tell who is trustworthy?"

It is frustrating when people we thought were reliable let us down or don't keep their word. If we're burned too often, we can find it hard to trust anyone. What's even more confusing is that some people are trustworthy in some situations but not in others. They show up on time but can't keep a secret, or they forget a dinner date but are always there in an emergency. Maybe I'm expecting too much or not communicating clearly. I don't know what to think.

> *There's a fine line between* caution and distrust.

> *Starting Point*
>
> Distrust to trust has a range from 1 to 10. A first meeting can never be more than a 3 because you still don't know that person. Trust is gained with time and experience.

5

Not Belonging

Sidelined

Maria:

I don't fit in. Everyone is so different from me. I can't connect to anyone. I don't understand what it is like to be part of a group. To feel a connection like others seem to. Even in my own family. Ha! Especially in my own family.

Then I wonder is it me or is it them? Are any of us really part of anything or anyone else?

Holly:

At times, we can feel awkward, out of place. Maybe we're new to a town where everyone else seems to have known each other all their lives. Or we may not look like most of the people we know, or our customs may seem strange to them. What if we're Yankees fans living in Boston? All these differences can make us feel like outsiders.

If we want to belong, how can we make that happen without losing our sense of who we are? If we don't want to belong, are we at peace with that, or is this just not the right place for us?

Andrea:

Sometimes in a careless way, we are brushed aside. The pressure of the busy lives of others, feeling forgotten or overlooked, not being called on, not being included, not being invited. The list is dangerously long. It has such sharp teeth. Once, in third grade, I had gone to the bathroom before a school outing. Others had as well. Suddenly, where had I been? Thinking? Daydreaming? I came out and realized that there was no one left in the bathroom. The school hall was empty. They had left. They had left me. I had such a deep feeling of sadness, of dread, of panic all at once. The brain is hardwired for belonging. I did not know that then. I just knew that I had been a part of something and suddenly was not. Was I not worth waiting for? The teacher would blame me for being too slow.

> *There's a fine line between* being different and feeling left out.

Starting Point

Do you want to belong, or do you not want to belong? Know yourself first, and then decide from there. Once you know what you want, you will be clearer about the groups you'd like to be with and how much you'd like to be with them. This is about you, not them.

6

Gridlock

Stuck

Holly:

There are many ways to be stuck. We can be stuck in a job that doesn't pay enough or that we don't like, stuck in an unhealthy relationship, stuck in a cycle of self-destruction, or simply stuck on the couch, unsure about what to do next.

Sometimes, much as we'd like to, we can't immediately fix what's wrong because of circumstances out of our control, an illness in the family, for example. But what about when we can see a way to change things for the better but are blocked at every turn? Do these obstacles mean that we are on the wrong track and should stop trying? Are they signs that the timing isn't right? Or are they problems that we need to solve before taking the next step? We are tangled up in all these threads.

Andrea:
Sometimes it is hard to see when we are stuck. It is not that we are stuck doing the same thing over and over. Far worse, we falsely believe that nothing—no action, no thought, no word—can change any aspect of our

lives. Our expectations hold us captive while the reality is too raw to face. We are frozen in a nightmare of our own making.

Maria:

I so desperately want to change my situation and life but I see no options for me. It's the same, every day. Nothing changes and nothing I can do will change anything. I can't imagine this is my forever.

> *There's a fine line between* thinking and stalling.

Starting Point

Treading water still counts as movement. You've got to start somewhere, so pick something small and do it.

7

Controlled in a Relationship

Bound and Gagged

Andrea:

To be controlled is to lose our personal freedom to another, to a concept, to a substance. Sometimes this loss occurs in microscopic amounts over time. Sometimes we can feel devoured. There is no oxygen that is ours. We blur into the other's needs too exhausted to stake any claim over any single part of our hopes or wants.

Maria:

I am an adult. But I have no power.

They don't see how stifled they make my life. How few choices I have because I always want to avoid their reactions. I dread their reactions. It is a strange feeling, a sad one, not to be free to do or say what is natural to me because there may be a reaction. Never knowing what will cause it so trying to stay small and quiet and hope that will be enough.

Holly:
It sneaks up on us. First "I don't think your friends like me," then "Why do you spend so much time with your friends"? and finally "I don't want you hanging out with your friends every

week." Giving up friendships is not enough. Next, we give away a beloved pet and ultimately cut ties with family members. Our world shrinks, and the relationship becomes our world. We make excuses for our controllers—they're just shy, they don't like dogs or are allergic to cats, and you have to admit my family hasn't been very welcoming—until we become the person we're expected to be rather than who were really are.

Giving in to controlling behavior doesn't work in the long run because the control never stops. Our wanting to save the relationship at all costs leaves us socially, financially, and personally exhausted, straining on a short leash. We need to find a safe way out before it's too late.

> *There's a fine line between* control and abuse.

> *Starting Point*
> This process happened slowly, and untangling it will take time, with small steps and support.

8

Inadequate

Thinking We're Not Good Enough

Maria:

People are funny. They often don't realize how hard their words are on someone.

"Don't be stupid!"

"You did WHAT!?!"

"You've got to be kidding…"

Messages that slowly erode us.

We can believe in things we cannot see but we can't believe in ourselves. Is this because we have been told about our value, our worth and capabilities and believe it when we are under-valued, called worthless and are told we are incapable?

Deep inside ourselves, deep inside, we know we are capable, worthy and valuable. We just need to figure out how to get it to the surface.

Holly:

"My sister wants me to sing at her graduation party, but I don't think my voice is good enough no matter what she says."

"Three months after a promotion at work, I'm still unsure of myself even though my boss says I'm doing a great job."

Sometimes we aren't good enough for a specific task because we aren't trained for it. Asking an electrician to perform brain surgery wouldn't end well, and asking a brain surgeon to rewire the house would likely involve the fire department. But most situations aren't that straightforward, and that's the problem.

The trick is knowing the difference between really not being good enough and just being afraid that we're not good enough.

Andrea:

Voices at home crushing him. The knife-point pain of each gray sticky name being glued to him so he could drag them all with him wherever he went. Everyone would know. Everyone could see who he wasn't. Everyone.

> *There's a fine line between* knowing our limits and limiting ourselves.

Starting Point
Remind yourself of your skills, and remember that there was a time when you hadn't learned them. You may not be able to do everything, but you can do more.

9

Faking Good

Imposter

Holly:

"I may look like the other managers at the conference, but they all have years of experience and I'm new. I hope it doesn't show."

"You think I know what I'm doing, but I have no clue how to calm my colicky baby."

Confidence is a handy mask for our insecurities. It may fool others, although we're not always positive about that, but it doesn't fool us. Yes, we may look the part and say all the right things, but deep down we know we are imposters. No one can convince us otherwise.

But what if we're wrong about that? Maybe we really are those people we think we're pretending to be. At some point will we be able to trust who we are?

Andrea:

Faking is a bad idea. It is driven by fear, and it is a part of much that we experience day to day. The talk is about "genuine" but the behavior, attitudes, and beliefs can be fake. Being fake metastasizes into false relationships, false impressions, a false self in all of our interactions. Misery usually follows.

What about sports performance, or other competitions in which you talk yourselves into excellent performance? Self-motivation and faking are different. I want to do well because it means something to me is very different from I have to do well or others will know who I am not.

Maria:

I messed up. I messed up and everyone knows. I know. I shouldn't have tried. What made me think I could do this and NOT mess it up? I should have known I would screw up. I thought I could manage this simple thing. It was simple. I can't even do a simple job without it becoming a disaster. I am useless.

> *There's a fine line between* confidence and self-doubt.

Starting Point

Are you sure that you even want this role? If your role feels uncomfortable, you may not have been given enough information or training or have an accurate view of what the role entails.

10

Feeling Out on a Limb

Exposed

Andrea:

One time I had to give a short but heartfelt presentation at a benefit. The number of people did not intimidate me but the high-volume crowd conversation did. I was trying to speak over the chatter and gallantly kept trudging on. It was so uncomfortable. I could not be my own advocate for silence without appearing unpleasant. I had always been able to self-advocate, but this time I did not have the freedom to do so. I felt very exposed. I could not defend my position. About halfway through, a compassionate person in the crowd commanded everyone to be quiet so I could be heard. I was grateful for the kindness.

Maria:

How did I get here? What wrong turns did I take. What the f*** happened?! How can I fix this? I can't fix this, I don't even know how this happened. There is no way I can figure out how to get out of this.

No one will help me because I did this, it's not their problem.

I am responsible so I need to figure it out but I have no idea how.

Holly:

"All but two of our hospital unit staff are out sick tonight, and no replacements are available. My coworker, who is a new nurse, and I have 46 very sick patients between us, and I worry we won't be able to provide good enough care."

"I'm about to give a sales presentation to a new client when my laptop freezes. Without my slides, I have to present the information from memory without making a fool of myself."

"I'm a strong ocean swimmer, but last week I was caught in a rip tide and dragged a long way before I got myself back to the beach. It turns out that a rip tide warning had been issued, but I hadn't bothered to check."

Clammy fear. Sometimes even panic. It can feel like that when we're taken by surprise and find ourselves in an exposed position, sometimes beyond our control. We are unprepared and are forced to think quickly.

This experience may be an obstacle or an opportunity, or both. There is much to learn from these lightning strikes.

> *There's a fine line between being uncomfortable and feeling abandoned.*

> *Starting Point*
>
> Acknowledge that you are in a difficult situation. Discomfort is part of the experience. Now is not the time to solve the problem, but remember that the problem is finite.

11

Out of Breath

Being Overwhelmed

Maria:

Oh boy. Let me get through today. I hope I can do that. I can't find a thought in my own head. It feels like scrambled eggs in there. One thing leads to a thousand and I can't do a thousand things. I can't even do the one. Or any. How can I get anything done. There's too much. How and where to start because there is no end.

Holly:

"The local paper ran an article about

my birthday cakes, and now I'm swamped with orders. I'm glad to have the business, but it feels like I'm running a marathon with a sprained ankle."

"We have full-time jobs, one child in first grade and another in middle school, and my father just had a major stroke and is coming to live with us. Last night I dreamed I ran away to Australia."

"The apartment building where I've lived for 20 years was sold, and I have a month to find a pet-friendly place I can afford. Where to begin?"

Being overwhelmed is a very personal condition. What is overwhelming to one person may be barely noticeable to another because we all have different minds, bodies, and experiences. But the feeling of being overwhelmed is universal, whatever the cause. The key is finding a way to manage it.

Andrea:

For many years after my mother died, I could remember that spring morning. I was watching the snow falling outside of our kitchen window, plump slowly meandering flakes. They had all the time in the world. My mother did not, although I did not know that then. It was Easter Sunday. She would die that night. It took me years to acknowledge that she no longer walked the earth. I felt buried under that snow.

> *There's a fine line between* the next to the last straw and the last straw.

> *Starting Point*
> When we are startled, anxious, or overwhelmed, we tend to hold our breath. First breathe out, and then take a normal breath. Keep repeating this sequence.

12

Cornerstones

Holding Up the World

Holly:

"I just keep going, but I wish there was a way to make this easier."

"I do what I have to do. I have a household to support."

We may live in an unstable world of constant change, but we still have responsibilities. At work, at home, in all aspects of our lives, we worry that if we aren't perfect enough, if we don't push ourselves hard enough, things will fall apart. One late payment can lower a credit score and lead to denial of an apartment or mortgage application. Staying home with a sick child can cost us our job. The stakes are high, and even if we do everything right, there's no guarantee that things won't fall apart, or that we won't. Many of us have shouldered this load willingly, even eagerly, but carrying it year after year can be exhausting, especially if we carry it alone.

Andrea:
When I quit drinking my deepest fear was that I would fail my friends, that they were counting on me to be the person I was when I drank. I, and they, had a vision of "me," but that thinking

had tricked me. My identity had become defined not by my beliefs, but by what I thought others needed of me. It felt wonderful to find out that I was finally able to be me.

Maria:

No one understands what my responsibilities are like. I have to keep going or else everything falls apart. EVERYTHING!

I can't take one minute for myself, people don't understand. I take one minute and nine things go wrong and then it takes me so much longer to get caught up and it isn't worth it.

No one gets it because they have no idea about my life.

> *There's a fine line between* responsibility and burden.

Starting Point
If there's any change you can make, move toward making it. If you've done whatever you can, remember to be easy on yourself.

13

Disappointment

Not Again

Andrea:

Recently I decided to see how people remembered any interactions we had in those early hours after a major event, in this case 9/11. Within minutes of the first attack, I had called my good friend, who was in sales. He was on the road at the time. I was the first to tell him and he said he "needed a visual" and went to a fast-food restaurant to find one. Years later he would say he did not remember my telling him, not at all. Right after the second attack, I had gone to see my sister because I was afraid I would not see her again. No one at the time, an hour or so after the event, knew what was going to happen. So much uncertainty, sadness, and fear. I went to her workplace to tell her I loved her. She told me recently she had no memory of that encounter. I was in the expectations-disappointment trap again! We expect something to be memorable to others because it is memorable to us, which is not always the case. We count on a shared moment being remembered in the same way and with the same feelings. This can create enormous disappointment for us. I was sad because they had not remembered me in a moment in which I remembered them. Clearly it was not as important in the same way to them, but I realized there can be so many reasons for that. The reminder is that those reasons may not be personal.

Maria:

I know they think I could do better. I know they think I'm not trying. I know they are disappointed in me.

Sure they say all the nice things to me but you can tell what they really think by the tone of their voice. The tone says "Why did we even hope or waste our time thinking you could."

It's like they don't think I want better for myself. Or worse, they don't think that I could be happy where I am because I could do better.

The disappointment runs both ways.

Holly:

"I was sure this time would be different."

"I should know better than to count on you."

We start with high hopes, or at least some hope, that we'll finish what we start, or do what we promised, or be where we need to be. Sometimes it works, but all too often we're distracted, pulled in another direction, and our plans fall apart. Again. So we keep trying. Another new day, another new beginning, fingers crossed that we won't disappoint ourselves or someone else this time.

Over time, we lose as much faith in ourselves as others do in us. Why does this keep happening? It could be that some of the people we disappoint have unrealistic expectations. We may also have unrealistic expectations about ourselves. Maybe we're not good at time management, we overcommit, or things take longer than estimated. We may have trouble saying no. Maybe we no longer want to do what we originally agreed to do. Or we're overwhelmed by all we've taken on and are too embarrassed or ashamed to admit it. We may not know the reason, but we want to change this pattern.

> *There's a fine line between* being disappointing and being disappointed.

> *Starting Point*
> Is this personal? It may not be, but check with those involved.

14

Grudge Holding

Maria:

I hate him.

How could I not hate him.

Nobody can blame me for hating him.

If they understood what happened they would hate him too.

Anytime I hear his name or see him it all comes back as if it was yesterday.

I could never forgive him. And his family doesn't seem to care at all. They are just like him. I hate them all.

And my "friends" they act like it was nothing. Asses. I hate them.

I will never forget and I will never forgive any of them.

I will use all my time and energy making sure I stay miserable.

Holly:

When someone has offended us or injured us or betrayed our trust, we are justified in being upset. But the sad fact is that the person who harmed us has probably moved on and may even have forgotten all about what happened. We are alone in our suffering.

Some of us spend a lifetime being offended, but it doesn't fix anything, and years of outrage can hold us hostage. We have a choice: hold the grudge tightly or let it go, recite the same story or write ourselves a new one. This sounds easier than it is. We are still hurting and may not be ready to put the grudge aside, at least not yet.

Andrea:

Focused, wary, holder of the scorecard. Why would we remember the harms that have been done? Mentally, we check it, that scorecard, either pretty regularly or as needed. What determines that is how much we feel threatened by any previous players. It is a game, after all, and requires a lot of mental energy. Who is paying for all that mental fuel? We are—the grudge holders. The grudge becomes worse in our minds, the price tag for holding it gets greater, the consequences to us get more powerful, more negative. Who will win? Over time who wins is not important and in most ways becomes irrelevant.

> *There's a fine line between* resentment and release.

> *Starting Point*
> Who is benefiting from this grudge? What would happen if you let it go?

15

Passing Up a Chance

Not Now

Holly:

"Great idea, but I don't see how this could work right now."

"I'm not sure I'm able to do this."

It doesn't happen often. In fact, it may happen only once or twice in a lifetime. We are given an opportunity that would change our lives for the better if we accepted it but wouldn't change a thing if we turned it down. It could be a job we want, or school, or even a relationship. Do we reach out and take the golden apple? No, but why not? Maybe we don't know what to do with it, or the timing is wrong, or we're not sure we're able to make this shift. Accepting this offer could turn our lives upside down. Maybe the job requires a cross-country move, the course of study will put us in debt, or the relationship will cause a family rift. It's also possible we're afraid of change, and saying no is easier than facing that fear. Whatever the reason, we walk away and get on with our lives. Over the years, we sometimes wonder what it would have been like if we had said yes. Next time, if there is a next time, can we find our way to yes?

Andrea:

At the age of 18, I told my father that I wanted to go and teach in a remote part of the world. He did not think I was mentally or emotionally equipped at that time to do that.

At 18, I did not hear the YET piece, maybe because I didn't want to. I didn't go, and I believe he may have been correct at that point in time. I never revisited that idea. I often wonder if we should have a light non-list way of checking back every few years to see not only whether we want to do something we didn't but to see where the idea went and what became of that part of us that wanted it. Does the idea appeal to us still, and if not, why not? Did we give up a part of ourselves by not doing it?

Maria:

Can I do this? It would be so wonderful, A chance to change things for the better. Or at least to change from where I'm at now. But so much would change. So much would have to change. There are so many decisions I would have to make and so much to consider.

Can I do this? It may not be the right time. I don't think I can handle it. There would be so many decisions to be made to make it all work. I don't know.

Maybe I better wait. Yeah, waiting is easier. Not so scary.

> *There's a fine line between* slamming a door shut and leaving it ajar for later.

Starting Point

Are you really interested in this or something like it? The original opportunity may have been missed, but a similar opportunity may be available in the future. There are doors that you may still be able to open.

16

Trapped

No Way Out

Andrea:

There are many ways in which we can't see other options in a situation. Boredom in relationships is one of them. We think we are in a situation that will never change, that we will rinse and repeat the same negative experiences until we shrivel up and die. It is hard to think of ways to change when we feel trapped. The very idea of thought can become a trap in and of itself.

Maria:

F***

F***

I got nothin'.

No idea. No f***in' idea what to do.

F***

What am I going to do.

Crap.

F***

Holly:

"I hate my job, but I need the health insurance for my sick child."

"This apartment is falling apart, but my credit isn't good enough to move right now."

"Is this how my life is always going to be, barely getting by, no time off, my relationship just hanging on?"

When life feels hopeless, how can I find a way to believe it will get better? And what can I do to make it better?

> *There's a fine line between* hope and despair.

> *Starting Point*
> Go from hopeless to hopeful one half-hour at a time. There's no need to think long term. These are the times for short-term thinking.

17

All My Fault

Blaming Ourselves

Maria:

I did it again. Ah yes, once more, a brilliant idea, a brilliant move and once more a colossal failure.

I can't get it right. I don't ever get it right. I don't even have the brains to recognize I should stop trying.

Oh, I can recognize when it's crashing and burning but do I learn. Of course not. What is wrong with me.

Holly:

"I should never have said that."

"I'll never forgive myself."

Guilt moves in and will stay as long as we let it. It keeps us stuck in a loop of shame and regret. But when we've done something wrong, what's the alternative to feeling guilty? Being accountable.

We all make mistakes, some of them possibly serious or permanent. Although we can't change what happened in the past, we can take responsibility for what we said or did, and we can try to make amends if possible and resolve to do better in the future. We can also start working toward accepting ourselves. How do we begin?

Andrea:

Every time I have said it was all my fault, it definitely was. There was never anything heroic in any of my stories, like taking the blame for a friend. I have stood up for an underdog or two, but that was because others were at fault and the person was being made to suffer. All the personal self-blame I have experienced occurred when I did not stand up to those who had strong opinions but were actually misinformed. It is a disjointed feeling when we stand, sit, kneel, or are crushed by the consequences of not standing up. One time I was in another country and saw a man carrying two twin mattresses on his back. This is what he did all day. This was his job. His upper body was parallel to the ground. This is much like the weight of self-blame. Can we ever stand straight again?

> *There's a fine line between* feeling guilty and being accountable.

Starting Point

Are you really to blame? If not, then it may not be your fault. If so, have you tried to make amends? Do you think it could make a difference?

18

Hedging

Am I Sure?

Holly:

"As soon as I make a decision, I worry that it was the wrong one."

"Looking at my past relationships, it's not surprising I don't trust my judgment when it comes to love."

"The upcoming move seemed like such a good idea. Now I'm not so sure."

Doubting ourselves isn't always a bad thing. A little doubt lets us weigh the pros and cons of a decision we're considering. But when we are overloaded with doubt, we don't trust ourselves to make good decisions, and we worry ourselves into insomnia over our choices. I want to earn my own trust and start believing in myself.

Andrea:

Often, and especially as time passes, family members and friends will remember the same shared events very differently. In its extreme, as an adult, an older brother may remember an early life of parents' fighting, drinking, barbed wire silences. A younger sister, when grown, may claim that the same childhood was magical, fun, full of happiness. Is someone lying, or is it just a matter of what we may want to remember? Two things can be true at the same time, and both may be right and true. It is easy to blame ourselves when we have the harder part to play in what we remember as the more painful past.

Maria:

Yeah! This is going to be great. It is going to be so epic. I am so excited. Everyone is going to love it!

Well, not everyone may be on board but almost all of them are. There may be a few hiccups but it'll be fine. Yes! It is going to be great.

They did bring up that one potential snag. Hmmm, if there is one there is always another. Then it's no longer a success but a bomb.

Maybe I should rethink this. Maybe, I should cancel.

> *There's a fine line between* doubt and belief.

Starting Point

Sound familiar?

A: What movie do you want to watch?

B: What do you want to watch?

A: I don't care. I chose last time.

B: I don't know. Hmmm. What do you feel like watching?

A: Just decide.

This happens a lot. Next time, take a chance and choose.

19

Overdoing It

"No Problem"

Andrea:

One time I worked 16 hours a day for three months. When my dad came to visit me and heard my self-imposed work schedule, he said: "I missed it!" When I asked what he had missed he said: "The monument with your name on it." His point was that it was a positive to work well, but no human being is supposed to be all things to any employer. The difference between working and over-working, between offering to help and overextending those offers is less noticeable to us once we have the habit of overextending. Then we are attached to the overextending, and it can be very hard to get off that stage.

Maria:

Day 1, hour 1: "Can you pick up something at the store for me?"
"Of course."

"Can you help me move a dresser later?"
"Sure."

"Will you come over today and get those things?"
"Absolutely."

"Would you be able to pick up my kids today?"

"I'd love to."

"This paperwork is impossible. Could you help me today?"

"Yes, don't worry."

Holly:

"Sure, I can fit this in."

"I'm pretty busy this week, but what's one more thing?"

Maybe we don't like saying no, maybe we underestimate how long a task will take, or maybe we like being heroes, but for whatever reason, we agree to do something that we will end up regretting because we don't have the time or the energy to do it without disrupting our lives. (This isn't about being overworked by a demanding employer. That is a whole different story because we often don't have a choice if we want to keep the job.)

Over time, others come to depend on our desire to please. We become known as reliable, able to step in when no one else will. At this point, even when we wisely say no and mean it, others don't always hear it, or they don't believe it. Being overridden is frustrating, and it needs to change.

> *There's a fine line between* just enough and too much.

> *Starting Point*
>
> Practice Nos.
>
> "No, thank you."
>
> "I am sorry but I can't."
>
> "I appreciate the offer, but I am unable to do it."
>
> "No way."

20

Life Is Flat

Maria:

Coulda, shoulda, woulda.

My life's good, great, I'm happy but maybe…

Coulda, woulda, shoulda.

Damn. Did I miss something?

What could I have done?

What would I do differently?

What should I do now.

Holly:

"There's nothing really wrong with my life, but sometimes it feels empty, and I don't know why."

"I keep thinking I should be doing something else."

When something seems missing, the odds are that something is. But what? That perfect life you worked so hard for and think you wanted may be someone else's idea of perfect, not yours. In fact, you may not want perfection at all anymore. At some point, you probably made a bargain with yourself that if you did everything that was expected of you, happiness would follow. Maybe it did at first, but settling for less has a heavy cost that comes due years later as a void you can't fill.

Some people choose to sidestep the

issue and make impulsive changes. The classic quick divorce, sports car, discarded friends, and unfamiliar lifestyle are not the answer if there's no real thought behind them. Sometimes our lives don't need a complete overhaul, just a few adjustments and a new way of looking at ourselves. If the goal is a more fulfilling life, then it's worth taking the time to learn what that means, and it's different for each of us.

Andrea:

When something seems missing in our lives, it probably is. There can be a lot of confusion, frustration, and even sometimes dread over the missing piece. We stir a lot up looking for it and take many paths to find it. What we sometimes forget in the search is that we usually don't have to ignore what we have in order to find what we need.

> *There's a fine line between* itching and scratching.

> *Starting Point*
> Life can seem flat. How are you going to make waves? Will they drown others? Will they drown you?

21

Influenza

Not Recognizing Our Influences

Holly:

"I've never liked the color pink."

"Deep water makes me nervous."

"For some reason, I like crooked teeth."

Do we always know why we like or dislike something? Do we even think about it? Sometimes the answer is close to the surface. I probably dislike pink because, as a child, it reminded me that I didn't fit in with other girls because I never had pink clothes. At age five, I was in a serious flood, so that explains the fear of water. But liking crooked teeth? I have no idea.

Once we figure out where these likes and dislikes come from, we can decide whether to keep them. Maybe we don't need them anymore. Maybe they were never really ours to begin with. The fun is in finding out.

Andrea:

Beaches are so beautiful. Towel on the sand, we move into the water and play. After a while, we get out of the water and our towel is quite a distance away. The current carried us away from our entry point, and we didn't even notice. Influence in our lives can have a similar effect. We can adapt to circumstances and people that are beneficial to us or to those that are less so. Adaptation can be subtle. By degree, we can learn more about ourselves, or begin to drift from our truest self.

Maria:

Be thin (don't be proud of who you are).

Get rich (you never have enough).

Look young (with our products).

Be healthy (with our drugs).

Have a family (the kind we want you to).

Listen to us (forget how you feel or what you think).

> *There's a fine line between* what's truly ours and what's not.

> *An instance...*
>
> When a woman who is now in her eighties was seven years old, she walked into a birthday party and overheard one of the adult guests ask the host, "And who is that very plain child?" To this day, she has never entered a room full of people without hearing that question in her head.

> *Another instance…*
>
> I always break spaghetti in half before I cook it. The other day, my mother asked me why I did that. I said, "Because you always did it." She laughed and said, "That was only to make it easier for you to eat it when you were little."

22

Overhelping

Andrea:

When we overhelp we prevent others from finding their way in the world. Helping does not have that effect, but overhelping does. We preempt other people's lives when we mandate, direct, and influence others to find or follow what we have found or believe. Overhelping is sticky, there is an agenda. So different from the lighter qualities of offering and suggesting that are the features of helping.

Maria:

What would they do without me? Honestly, thank goodness I am here for them. They don't realize how much they need me but at least I do and am more than happy to make life easier for them. Poor things, they keep saying "no," that they're fine but really? Are they?

I don't think so. I have so much more experience than they do. I would have loved it if I had had me in my life when I was in their situation.

They are lucky that I don't listen to them.

Holly:

"Here, let me help you with that."

"Isn't helping other people a good thing?"

With the best of intentions, we offer to help someone we know who is having a difficult time. A neighbor has just had a knee replacement. We pick up groceries, run some errands, and drive to physical therapy appointments.

Before we know it, weeks turn into months. Our neighbor has recovered and was cleared to drive last month but still doesn't feel ready. We worry that too much helping may be making our neighbor helpless. Now what?

> *There's a fine line between* being kind and creating dependence.

> *Starting Point*
> Before offering to help, ask yourself, "Can I take that on? Would it be too much for me?"

23

Staying Seated

Inaction

Maria:

I can't help. Not with this. What could I do? It would be pointless. I'm sure someone else is taking care of this. This is not something I need to get involved in. It would be a waste of my time in any case because I can't help.

Holly:

"I believe my boss was fired unfairly. I wanted to complain to higher management about it but was afraid I'd lose my job."

"Someone next to me on the bus started a conversation, but it became clear that this person's views and mine were totally at odds. My seatmate seemed to hate almost everyone and assumed I felt the same way. I was at a loss for words and later regretted staying silent."

"Out for a walk, I saw someone mistreating a dog. When I objected, the person gave me a dirty look and turned away with the dog. I keep asking myself whether I should have done more."

When we see or hear something wrong and say nothing, we are signaling agreement. Witnessing injustice or harm or hurtful speech calls for a response, but most cases are not as clear-cut as saving a baby or animal left in a hot car. What if we're in a parking lot and see an argument turn violent? Is it safe to say anything? We need to consider our safety and that of others. Should we call 911? Do we even know for sure what we're looking at? It's easy to convince ourselves to walk away when we're uncertain about what's happening. Knowing how to size up a situation is a valuable skill that, in the right circumstances, can help us overcome a natural tendency to silence and inaction.

Andrea:

We have a voice. When we don't use it we can erase ourselves into a dark silence. We use it to sing, we use it to soothe, we use it to tell our stories. It heals us. With it we can speak our truth. We can speak our truth to others. There are times when we should stay seated and times that we should stand.

> *There's a fine line between* outrage and action.

Starting Point

If you have to ask yourself, "Is this really happening to me?", it probably is. Acknowledging this is a first step toward changing inaction to action.

24

Caving to Convenience

Holly:

Convenience can stunt our growth. When we grab what's within reach, we don't stretch. Saying yes because it's simpler than explaining why we want to say no, giving in to pressure instead of standing our ground, staying silent to avoid conflict, doing what's easiest instead of what's best for us—these are all ways that we give convenience the upper hand in making our choices.

But what about when we're too exhausted or overwhelmed to do anything other than what we absolutely have to do, times when survival, not growth, is the goal? We cling to convenience because, at that moment, we need it. That's when sneering at convenience is unfair—and unkind.

How about this instead? At those times when we are able to dispense with convenience, it's worth a try.

Andrea:

The costliest lesson of caving to convenience is that we can lose ourselves. Our unwillingness to be clear with ourselves about defining our actions and intentions makes us erode our own edges. We need to be able to adapt to convenience when needed but at the same time to make decisions with an eye on their consequences to us and to others.

Maria:

It'll be okay. Yeah. It'll be fine. No problemo. It'll be alright. Okay, maybe there's a better way but this'll do. It'll be okay. Yeah. It'll be fine.

> *There's a fine line between* convenience and expedience.

> *Starting Point*
>
> Drive-throughs are popular for a reason, but are they the best option for us?

25

Hitting a Wall

Facing Loss

Andrea:

We often have to hit a wall before we realize that we may actually have been doing the best we could. That best was the best it could have been at that time. The revisiting of our past actions or behaviors as seen from the present is usually full of relentless scrutiny and self-berating. We learn and grow through time, and through hitting many walls. We become better.

Maria:

Gone. Forever.

What do I do now? Why? Why did this happen?

What do I do? I don't know what to do. Gone. Gone. Done. Oh my God. I can't move. I can't breathe. Please, please, no. Please. Why? Oh, please, no.

No hope. No future. Nothing. Darkness.

Holly:

Reeling from a major loss, we can find it hard to breathe in a life we may no longer recognize as our own. Joy is gone, color is gone, replaced by endless gray. We are exhausted, hollow. Telling ourselves that things will get better is no help at all because we have no way of knowing that. We need to find a way to get through the next day.

> *There's a fine line between* sorrow and depression.

> *Starting Point*
> No matter how tragic and painful the loss is, we need to sit in the wreckage of this loss and acknowledge it. This is first of several steps toward healing.

26

I Believe

Maria:

There is more than one side to everything.

People are naturally good.

It is easy to get stuck in a certain way of thinking.

Taking time to think about things is important.

I need to pay attention to where information comes from.

It is our purpose to improve and evolve.

Kindness is the key to happiness.

You can't change others only yourself.

Fear is the root of hatred.

I can change.

Holly:

"I tend to believe what I see on TV."

"I trust social media more than so-called mainstream news."

"My neighbor's cousin's friend is giving me a ride to the city so I don't have to spend nine hours on a bus. I don't know this person, but it will be OK, I guess."

Do we believe something because we want to or because it is true? It's not always easy to tell the difference because who we are influences what we believe. Is the truth somewhere between two extremes, or is it somewhere else? How can we recognize the truth and free it from the net of misinformation and lies?

Andrea:

One of the most important favors we can do for ourselves is to think through what we see and hear and come to our own conclusions. We can trick ourselves into thinking things that are not true, and if not careful we can get very stuck in that thinking. We may miss an important detail by overfocusing on what we want to hear or see. We pick the first door, just for convenience, forgetting about the other doors that may also have equally good or better options. Our closest interpretation is not always our best one.

> *There's a fine line between* truth and exploitation.

> *Starting Point*
> With information coming at us on all sides, it's hard to know what's true.

27

My Own Personal Obstacle

What is an obstacle that keeps me stuck, holds me back, or stands in my way? And why do I call it an obstacle?

Part II

Core Issues and Exercises

We've identified some core issues and have designed exercises related to these issues. Each exercise can help with one or more of the obstacles described earlier. Hang on, here they come!

A

Power and Control

Who holds your power, you or someone else? Do you hold someone else's power? If so, you probably don't realize you're doing it.

1. Empathy Exercises
    a. Volunteering
    b. Switching tasks or roles with someone else in the household
    c. Staying off your phone or social media for eight hours
2. Releasing Control

Do something (nothing illegal or harmful) you don't want to do ("I would rather die than …). See what happens.

3. Empowerment: Speaking Up

   a. In a neutral setting, such as a grocery store customer service desk or a library, start a one-on-one conversation (examples: asking whether something is in stock at the store, getting a library card).

   b. Be part of a conversation in a group setting with friends or family.

   c. Speak up in a setting in which you don't agree with someone.

4. Taking Control
    a. "I would die of embarrassment if I ...."
    b. Then experience it. You may be embarrassed, but you won't die.

B

Boundaries

Boundaries are about respect. Do you have personal boundaries? Do you know where they are? Do you let other people trespass? Are you a trespasser?

1. Respect for Others

    Ask yourself: "Am I asking someone to do something I wouldn't do myself (such as staying overtime at work)?"

2. Wanting Your Own Way

    "I want my way." A good example is "When are you going to give me grandchildren?" Think about what would happen if you didn't get your way. For one week, you may not make demands or give advice. Then follow up by saying, "I have not been paying enough attention to what you needed, only what I wanted." Listen to each answer.

3. Self-Respect

   Ask yourself: "Am I acting in a way that is respectful to me? Is what I'm doing showing respect for myself?" (The staying overtime example fits this question, too.)

4. Coping With Intrusion

   "I feel pressured. I want to make my own decisions." (This is after being asked, "When are you going to give me grandchildren?") Approach three people who have been making demands of you. Tell them that you are not sure you can do what they ask, and offer alternatives.

5. Learning to Say No

For one week, when asked to do something, say "I'm sorry I am not able to do it this time." Offer an alternative. You do not need to explain. (If you believe a refusal to do what's asked would be unwise, use your best judgment.)

C

Old Habits and Leftovers

1. Leftovers: Boxes in the Basement

   You probably have them, too—boxes you've been moving from place to place for so long you don't remember what's in them or why you still hang on to them. What would you find if you opened one? Band tee shirts? Your high school graduation program?

   It's not just old cardboard boxes that we carry around with us. We all have beliefs, likes and dislikes, fears, desires, and hopes, some so deeply embedded that we don't remember where they came from or why they are there. Each one is a box we can open and peek inside. Take fear of fire, for example. For someone badly burned in a wildfire, the source of that fear is obvious. But what if you're afraid of fire because your grandfather's house burned down when he was a child, and he told the story over and over again? That was his fear, not yours, and once you realize it, you don't have to hold onto it anymore.

The more boxes you open—whether these boxes are external or internal, the clearer you'll be about who you are now and what you truly believe.

2. Old Habits

   List five of your long-standing habits. Then ask yourself the following two questions for each habit: What does it keep me from doing? Do I want to change it? Write down your answers, and put them aside. A couple of weeks later, repeat the exercise. Do you still feel the same way? Has anything changed?

D

Self-Trust

Sometimes we are afraid of any decision we might make. This paralysis keeps us from looking at our options.

1. Bad Decisions
   a. When was the last time you made a bad decision, and what did you think happened as a result of that decision?
   b. What other decisions could you have made at that time?
   c. What could you choose now instead?
2. Staying Away From Decisions

a. Think about what you want to eat for dinner. Time yourself. You have five minutes to decide, and you can't change your mind. Bon appetit!

b. Arrange an outing with at least one other person. You decide the activity ahead of time. You can change the people you go with, but you can't change the outing. Enjoy!

3. Full Hand

a. On a sheet of paper, trace an outline of your hand, with fingers spread apart.

b. For each finger, and your palm, think of a positive quality of yours, and write it on the paper.

c. Keep the paper as a reminder to yourself.

E

Changing Limitations

When facing any problem, we have limited options. It may be hard to see any other options outside of these because the burden of the problem restricts our ability to see them. These limitations can highjack our lives. In some cases, these limitations are self-imposed.

Exploring Our Options

a. Choose something you are worried about.

b. Take a blank sheet of paper and write down all your options, even ones that seem impossible or strange.

c. Starting with one option, can you imagine a way to make it happen? Focus on the possibility. Don't let your usual way of thinking stand in the way. Where can you get more information on that option?

Example: My car, which I use to get to work, needs repairs I can't afford. What am I going to do? My list of all the options I can think of includes learning to repair it myself, bartering with a mechanic, limiting the use of the car, using public transportation, riding my old bicycle to work, carpooling with coworkers with similar hours, moving closer to work, or finding a different job. Looking at these options, I can see myself biking to work, at least until I can pay for the car repair, but just the act of writing "finding a different job" makes me smile.

F

Avoidance

We all like to feel comfortable, but it isn't always in our best interest. Avoidance doesn't make things go away. Don't turn the page to the next exercise—let's work on this now.

1. Having a Difficult Conversation (this doesn't have to mean an argument)
    a. Ask the other person their thoughts.
    b. Exhale before responding, and then keep your answer short.
    c. Rinse and repeat.

2. Dealing With an Awkward Situation
   a. Don't expect anything, either positive or negative.
   b. Go ahead and state the obvious: "This is awkward." See where that leads. Don't expect anything.
   c. Rinse and repeat.
3. Change
   a. What don't you want to change? What would happen if you changed it?
   b. What would happen if you didn't?

G

Making Choices

Pay attention to our choices when they arise. It often comes naturally to make choices automatically, out of habit, or for reasons that no longer make sense.

1. Present Choice
    a. Think of a choice.
    b. Do you care about it? Do you need to care about it? Why does it matter to you? Who else would care about it?
    c. Now think about the choice again.

2. Past Choice
    a. Think about a choice that you made in the past that you regret.
    b. Why do you regret it? Did you want to make that choice then? Were there any other options at that time?
    c. Can you find a way to see it differently?

H

Flexibility

How often have we said or heard this?

- We have always done it that way.
- That's the way it's always been.
- Why fix what isn't broken?
- I can't imagine doing it any other way.

It may be time to see, do, and think about things differently.

1. Getting Dressed
    a. Notice how you get dressed in the morning (or later, if you work at night).

b. The next day, change one thing (such as putting your socks on first or last).

c. The following day, change one more thing.

d. Stick with this new routine for another week.

2. Food for Thought

a. Think of a food you disliked as a child. Give it another try.

b. Try a new food or a new way of preparing a familiar food.

c. Change one of the side dishes or desserts you usually serve at a holiday gathering. See what happens, and have fun with that!

I

Acceptance

Sometimes we need to accept events and circumstances, as painful as they are. It can take time to do this, and it is an uncomfortable process, but valuable.

1. What You've Done: Taking Responsibility
   a. Think of some harm you have done, intentionally or accidentally.
   b. Accept what happened, and accept your role in it, You will probably feel worse than you do

now. Accept that as well.

c. Make amends without causing further harm. Amends can include apologies, restitution, and reparations. There may be times when it is not possible or allowed to make amends, or the amends may be rejected. We have to accept that, too.

d. In a way, you have to wake up to what you did. Only then can you change your behavior. Only then can you be alert to what you are doing.

2. What You've Done: Seeing It Differently

a. Write down two things that you firmly believe you can never forgive yourself for.

b. Now imagine that your friend, parents, or child came up to you and said the first of the two things you wrote down.

c. How would react, and what would you say to them?

3. What Someone Else Has Done

a. Think of some harm someone else has done to you or that affects you. Was it intentional or accidental?

b. If it was accidental, are you still angry about it? Sad? Resentful?

Does it matter to you that it was accidental? Even if it was an accident, there can be great anguish. It takes time for hurt and sorrow to heal themselves and to help us heal.

c. If someone has meant to harm you, do they know it? They may not see it the way you do. Is your focus on this incident interfering with your life or the lives of others around you? Payback is hell…on you.

4. When No One Is to Blame for Harm or Loss

a. If your safe structure has been destroyed, think about rebuilding it in your own way.
b. If your life has had a major upheaval, ask yourself, "What do I want, and what do I need?"
c. Small changes in your routine, your living space, what you eat, even what you wear can make a surprisingly large difference.

J
Appreciating

It is easy to fall into a trap of frustration in daily living. We don't believe that others can think clearly, we believe they are misguided, annoying, incompetent. But we can change that frustration by taking a different approach.

1. Rethinking Appreciation
    a. Pretend that you are in your car behind a person driving very very slowly in the passing lane!
    b. Think of three reasons they might be driving so slowly.

Start with "Maybe this person …."

Example "Maybe this person is upset because a family member died."

c. When you finish imagining the three reasons, silently wish the other driver well. No, really do it. Wish them joy and happiness in life. Then ask yourself why you are in such a rush. Are you afraid of disappointing some one? Do you believe you will be judged harshly? Will there be an argument? Will you feel powerless and hopeless as a result? Frustration is usually about perceiving something as a negative experience and reacting to it because it may be a factor in causing later emotional hardship or distress. Taking pressure off yourself and others helps you appreciate who you are and who you can be in the world.

2. Spreading Appreciation

Think of someone who you appreciate for their help, kindness, companionship, good work, anything. Tell them.

3. Simple Appreciation

Try to see the sunrise, or sunset, or moonrise as often as possible. Your day will begin and end with something beautiful that you don't have to make happen.

K

Clear Thinking

Every year tens of thousands of people are lured into loss of money through online romance scams. The pattern the scammers use is pretty well established. They cultivate trust and credibility. They pay compliments, they are helpful, caring. They get to "know" the person online and then they ask for funds for medical emergencies and other personal hardships.

We know this happens, it is widely publicized, yet people still fall for it.

Why? They are not thinking clearly. Their emotional needs outweigh their logic or "common sense." Their need to be valued and cared about is so much more attractive than the idea that they could be exploited. This override of emotional need over common sense or logic is very common any time we are not thinking clearly.

1. Be a Detective.

    Question everything. If you hear something and it seems incredible, it probably is, no matter where you heard it or read it, no matter who told you. Check the facts for yourself. Ask yourself WHY this item would be presented as a fact or event. What could be the motive? Even if the answers you come up with seem absurd, think about all possibilities as potential truths until the correct or most likely one emerges. Practice this in daily living until it becomes a good brain habit.

Example: Your son says Friday is a professional day and there is no school.

True? Not true? Fact check. No need to fact check, you say, your son would never lie. OK. Maybe someone told him there was no school and he didn't think clearly and is repeating a rumor! Could he have a motive for lying for the first time ever?? MOTIVE. He is in love with his girlfriend and she has begged him to skip school to go to the beach with her. Maybe he is tired of being a dutiful son and wants to break a rule. Finding the truth is an important part of clear thinking.

2. Check Your Sources

   a. What is your first impression of any information you read, see, or hear? Does it feel right? Does it make sense?

   b. Consider the source. Are you familiar with it? Has it been accurate in the past?

    c. Do you have outside confirmation or proof that this information is true? If not, be skeptical.

    d. Give yourself a few days and see whether you still feel the same way about it.

3. Be Careful

    a. Does this situation involve another person? How well do you know that person?

    b. Make sure someone else knows where you are going and with whom. If sharing that information bothers the other person, leave right away. That is a bright red flag.

c. Does this situation involve dangerous behavior on your part? If so, what's your reason for doing it? Is it your idea or someone else's?

d. Have you considered the consequences? Think before you leap.

Useful Resources

The following is a list of national organizations and hotlines that you can access if needed. Most communities also have local resources that may be helpful.

- 9-8-8 Suicide and Crisis Lifeline: Available 24/7 in English and Spanish. Call 988. See also https://988lifeline.org
- Heads Up Guys men's mental health information: www.headsupguys.org
- National Alliance on Mental Illness (NAMI): Call 1-800-950-

NAMI. Or text 62640 for Helpline. Monday to Friday 10 am to 10 pm. See also www.nami.org

- National Domestic Violence Hotline: Available 24/7 in English and Spanish. Interpreters for other languages available. Call 1-800-799-7233 (1-800-799-SAFE).
- Self-injury hotline: Call 1-800-DONTCUT (1-800-366-8288)
- Trevor Project LGBTQIA+ mental health information: www.thetrevorproject.org
- Veteran's Crisis Line: Call 988, then press 1. Or text 838255. See also www.veteranscrisisline.net

- Women's mental health information: www.safeproject.us

Acknowledgments

We thank everyone who has generously contributed to this book, through interviews, early readings, and sharing their struggles.

About Us

Andrea Facci – Loves helping those trying to reach their potential, is a friend of nature and its inhabitants, and committed to lifelong learning in herself and in others. Hope leads the way. Works as a licensed counselor. Maria is her sister. Holly is her friend.

Maria Facci likes to be creative in many different ways. She has worked a variety of jobs including several in the service industry.

Holly Lukens is an intuitive consultant, a medical editor and writer, and the author of *Show Me Yes: Divorce as a Learning Tool*.

Index

Acceptance, 157-161
Alienation, 23-26
Appreciating, 163-166
Autopilot decisions, 13-18
Avoidance, 151-152
Awkward situations, 151-152
Being overwhelmed, 51-54
Being stuck, 29-32
Beliefs, 123-126
Blaming ourselves, 79-82
Boredom, 95-98
Boundaries, 135-137
Boxes in the basement exercise, 139-140
Change exercise, 152
Changing limitations, 147-149
Choices, 13-17, 133-134, 141-142
Clear thinking, 167-172
Control and power, 33-36, 131-133
Convenience, 115-118
Core issues and exercises.129-172. *See also* specific exercises
    Acceptance, 157-161
    Appreciating, 163-166
    Avoidance, 151-152

    Boundaries, 135-137
    Changing limitations, 147-149
    Clear thinking, 167-172
    Flexibility, 155-156
    Making choices, 153-154
    Old habits and leftovers, 139-141
    Power and control, 131-133
    Self-trust, 143-145
Decision making, 13-18, 143-145, 153-154
Difficult conversations, 151
Disappointment, 59-64
Distrust, 19-22, 143-144
Doing too much, 89-93
Empathy exercises, 131
Empowerment, 132
Exercises, 129-172. *See also* Core issues and exercises; specific exercises
Exploring options, 147-149
Feeling burdened, 55-58
Feeling like an imposter, 41-44
Feeling exposed, 45-49
Feeling trapped, 75-77
Flexibility, 155-156
Food for thought exercise, 156
Getting dressed exercise, 155-156
Grudge holding, 65-68
Guilt, 79-82, 157-158
Habits, 141

Hand exercise, 144-145
Harm or loss, 119-121, 157-161
Helping too much, 105-108
Hopelessness, 75-77
Inaction, 109-113
Inadequacy, 37-40
Intrusion, 136-137
Invisibility, 9-12
Learning to say no, 93, 137
Limitation change exercise, 147-149
Loss or harm, 119-121, 157-161
Missed opportunities, 69-73
Not being heard, 5-8
Not being seen, 9-12
Not belonging, 23-27
Not trusting others, 19-22
Obstacles, 3-127
    Autopilot decisions, 13-18
    Being ignored, 5-8
    Being overwhelmed, 51-54
    Being stuck, 29-32
    Beliefs, 123-126
    Blaming ourselves, 79-82
    Boredom, 95-98
    Controlled in a relationship, 33-364
    Convenience, 115-118
    Disappointment, 59-64
    Facing loss, 119-121

    Feeling burdened, 55-58
    Feeling exposed, 45-49
    Feeling inadequate, 35-38
    Feeling like an imposter, 41-44
    Feeling trapped, 75-77
    Grudge holding, 65-68
    Guilt, 79-82, 157-158
    Hedging, 83-87
    Hopelessness, 75-77
    Inaction, 109-113
    My own personal obstacle, 127
    Not being heard, 5-8
    Not being seen, 9-12
    Not belonging, 23-27
    Not trusting others, 19-22
    Overdoing it, 89-93
    Overhelping, 105-108
    Passing up a chance, 69-73
    Self-doubt, 83-87
    Unrecognized influences, 99-103
    Opportunities missed, 69-73
Option exploration, 147-149
Overdoing it, 89-93
Overhelping, 105-108
Passing up a chance, 69-73
Power and control, 33-36, 131-133
Relationships, 33-36, 131-133, 135-137. *See also* specific issues

Releasing control, 131-132
Resource list, 173-175
Respect for others, 135
Self-doubt, 83-87
Responsibility, 55-58, 157-159
Self-respect, 136
Self-trust, 143-145
Taking control, 133
Thinking clearly, 167-172
Thinking we're not good enough, 37-40
Trust, 19-22, 143-145
Truth, 123-126, 167-172
Uncertainty, 83-87
Unrecognized influences, 99-103
Wanting your own way, 135-136

www.ingramcontent.com/pod-product-compliance
Lightning Source LLC
Chambersburg PA
CBHW070758020526
44118CB00036B/1904